Please return / renew this item by the last date shown above
Dychwelwch / Adnewyddwch erbyn y dyddiad olaf y nodir yma

…ners Ltd.
…ondon, W1D 3QY

…081-0851-2
…081-1287-8

…Gill Matthews

…009 Louise Spilsbury

…Spilsbury to be identified as the author of this work has been
…accordance with the Copyrights, Designs and Patents Act 1988.

…r this book is available from the British Library.

…ed using paper that is made from wood grown in managed,
…It is natural, renewable and recyclable. The logging and
…esses conform to the environmental regulations of the

…Black by Calcium.
…n China by C&C Offset Printing Co.

…esses given in this book were correct at the time of going to
…nd publishers regret any inconvenience caused if addresses
…es have ceased to exist, but can accept no responsibility for

…ts
…d like to thank the following for their kind permission to
…tographs:
…: Kurhan. **Pages:** Fotolia: Domenico Gelermo 12; Istockphoto:
…, Jiang Dao Hua 15t, Zlatko Kostic 18, Iris Nieves 19t;
…curs 21r, Cheryl Casey 6, Elena Elisseeva 5tl, Sonya Etchison
…des 5br, Frantisekhojdysz 11t, Fred Goldstein 10, Iofoto 21l,
…, Monkey Business Images 4, 5bl, 21cr, Morgan Lane
…hit Seth 21cl, Suravid throughout, Leah-Anne Thompson 7.
…erstock: Oguz Aral, Sebastian Kaulitzki; Geoff Ward.

Top B
Questi

Louise Spilsbury

Published 2009
A & C Black Pub
36 Soho Square
www.acblack.co

ISBN HB 978-
    PB 978-

Series consulta

Text copyright

The right of L
asserted by h

A CIP catalo

This book
sustainab
manufac
country

Produce
Printed

All the
press.
have
any s

Ackn
The
repr
Cov
Stud
Shu
5tr
21
Ph

Contents

How Do Bodies Work?

Did you know that the human body is the world's most amazing machine? It is made up of many different parts and although these parts do different jobs, they also work together to make the whole machine run smoothly.

What controls the body?

The human body is controlled by the **brain**, which acts like a powerful computer. It sorts information and controls how the body works. Messages between the brain and the rest of the body travel along **nerves**. For example, if you pick up something hot, nerves carry a message to the brain. Then the brain sends back a **signal** to your hand to tell you to move it. This is called the **nervous system**.

The brain sorts information at high speed, and sends messages around the body in a fraction of a second.

4

Why should you look after your body?

You should look after your body to keep it working properly.

Regular sleep gives the body a rest. However, one part of the body never sleeps – the brain. It continues working to control functions throughout the body, such as breathing.

Cars run on petrol and computers use electricity. The human body is fuelled by food. People need to eat a range of foods to help them stay healthy.

There is water in almost every part of the body, and the body needs water to function. People need to drink fresh water every day, because they lose water when they sweat or go to the toilet.

To keep healthy, you should also be active for an hour every day. As well as sports, this could include walking to school or helping with household chores.

5

What Does Skin Do?

The largest part of the human body is the skin. Human skin covers an area of almost 2 sq m (21.5 sq ft)! When you touch something, nerves beneath the skin send information to the brain.

Skin is like a warm, waterproof coat that protects everything inside.

Why is skin like body armour?

The layer of skin over the body is as useful as a suit of armour!

- It protects the heart and other important **organs** inside the body from bumps and knocks.

- Skin stops germs getting inside that could make you ill. The only way germs can get inside your skin is when it is scratched or cut.

- Skin helps to keep just the right amount of moisture in the body to work efficiently.

Why does skin sweat?

Did you know that most people lose 1 or 2 litres (up to 3.5 pints) of sweat a day, but athletes can lose up to 4 litres (7 pints) in an hour? People sweat to cool down. When the body is hot, sweat comes out of tiny holes in the skin's surface. Then the sweat dries in the air and takes some body warmth with it.

Your face goes red when you are hot because your blood vessels rise to the surface of your skin to cool you down. Your skin helps to warm you up, too. When it is cold, body hairs stand up. This traps a layer of warm air around your skin.

Why wash skin?

You need to wash skin to remove sweat, dirt, and germs. Germs are tiny living things that can make you ill if they get into your body.

Most germs spread through touching. That is why it is important to keep your skin clean.

Why Should You Brush Your Teeth?

You need to brush your teeth because teeth are the only parts of the human body that cannot repair themselves. Teeth are important for eating and for clear speech.

How often should you clean teeth?

People should brush their teeth for two minutes at a time, at least twice a day. This protects the white **enamel** on the tooth's surface. Enamel is very hard so it protects the more sensitive parts inside the tooth. However, a substance called plaque can burn holes in enamel and give you toothache. Plaque forms when sugars in food stick to teeth, and bacteria (germs) gather in the sugar.

Sweets and other sugary foods may look good, but they can harm your teeth.

Snack attack

Use this list to choose snacks that won't harm your teeth.

Healthy	Harmful
Bread or pretzels	Cakes
Carrots	Fizzy drinks
Cheese and milk	Sweetened cereals
Plain yoghurt	Sweets
Nuts and seeds	

What are milk teeth?

Milk teeth grow while you are still a baby and drinking milk. Children usually have about 20 milk teeth by the time they are three years old. From about six years old, milk teeth start to drop out and new permanent teeth grow in their place. Permanent teeth have to last a lifetime.

You can build strong teeth by eating foods that contain calcium. The body uses calcium to make enamel.

Why are teeth different shapes?

Teeth are different shapes so they can cut, chew, and grind different foods.

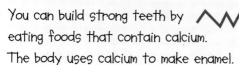 Incisors are the four front teeth that have sharp straight ends for cutting through food. You have two at the top and bottom of your mouth.

Canines are the four sharp and pointed teeth on each side of the incisors. Canine teeth grab and tear food.

At the back of your mouth are molars. These teeth have flat, wide tops for crushing and grinding food to make it ready to swallow.

9

Why Do People Sneeze?

When people sneeze, air comes out of their nose at 150 kmh (95 mph). That is faster than cars speeding along a motorway!

Why do sneezes happen?

When you breathe in germs, smoke, or dirt they stick to little hairs and mucus (snot) inside the nose. This tickles the nose hairs and sends a signal to the brain. The brain then tells the body to take an extra big breath and blow them out in a sneeze.

When you have a cold your nose makes extra mucus to soak up the germs.

How do noses smell?

Your nose gives you your sense of smell. Inside the nose there are over 10 million tiny scent **receptors**. They can smell the tiny **particles** that you breathe in with the air. Then the receptors send information about the smells to the brain.

How does breathing work?

To breathe, people take in air through their nose and mouth. Then this air travels down into the lungs. The lungs take **oxygen** from the air and pass it into the blood. The blood delivers oxygen to all of the other parts of the body. The body uses oxygen to release energy from the food people eat. The body needs energy to stay alive, grow, and repair itself.

We must breathe all the time. That is why divers carry oxygen supplies with them underwater.

Why is smoking bad?

When people use cigarettes they take smoke into their lungs. This can cause serious health problems:

🖐 Smoking can cause lung cancer when you get older.

🖐 Smoking makes you cough and affects your breathing.

🖐 Smoking affects your senses of smell and taste.

11

Why Do People Blink?

Did you know that most people blink around 15,000 times a day, without really noticing it? Blinking produces tears that help to keep the surface of the eye moist and clean.

Why are tears useful?

Tears are made by parts called glands in the upper eyelids. Every time people blink, a tear leaves the glands. It washes onto the eye through tiny holes called tear ducts.

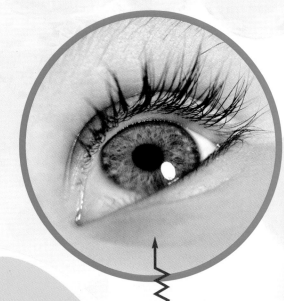

Eye care

 Wear sunglasses. This helps to prevent sun rays damaging the eyes.

Take regular computer breaks so you don't strain your eyes.

Wear safety goggles when you do activities like woodwork.

Read in good light, because your eyes strain to see in dim light.

Blinking helps to wash dirt and dust out of the eye.

12

How do eyes work?

1. When people look at an object, light reflects or bounces off the object into the eyes.

2. The light passes through the pupil, which is the black bit in the middle of an eye.

3. When the patterns of light hit the back of the eye, a part called the retina changes them into signals.

4. Finally, the signals travel to the brain so that it can tell you what you are looking at.

Why do you have two eyes?

People have two eyes so they can do things like catch a ball, pick up a pen, and see things all around. Each eye sees slightly different views of what you are looking at. Looking at something with one eye gives you a flat, two-dimensional view of the object. The brain combines the different views from both eyes to give you a single three-dimensional image. That tells you how far away an object is and whether it is closer or further away than another object.

Two eyes give you a three-dimensional view of something and tell you how close or far away an object is.

13

How Do Ears Work?

Did you know that the flap of skin we call the ear doesn't actually hear? Sounds make the air vibrate. The ear picks up these **sound waves** and sends them through a complicated obstacle course all the way to the brain!

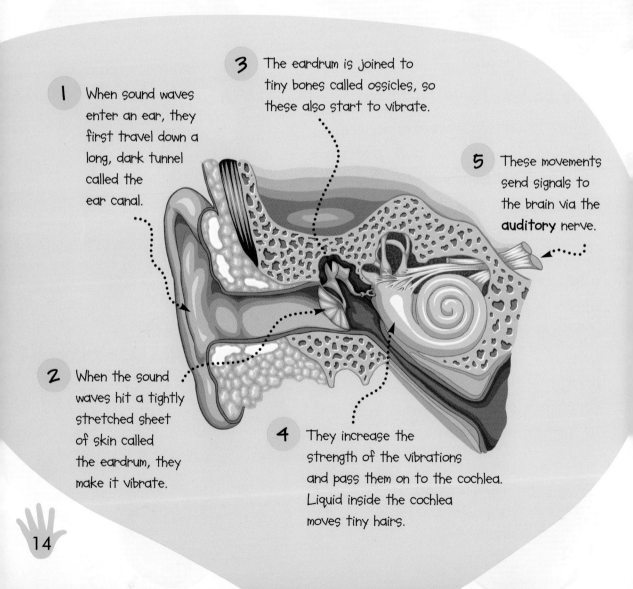

1 When sound waves enter an ear, they first travel down a long, dark tunnel called the ear canal.

3 The eardrum is joined to tiny bones called ossicles, so these also start to vibrate.

5 These movements send signals to the brain via the **auditory** nerve.

2 When the sound waves hit a tightly stretched sheet of skin called the eardrum, they make it vibrate.

4 They increase the strength of the vibrations and pass them on to the cochlea. Liquid inside the cochlea moves tiny hairs.

How do ears help with balance?

Did you know that as well as helping you to hear, ears also help you to balance? Inside the ear there are bony tubes containing fluid. When you move, the fluid also moves. The brain interprets the fluid movements to help keep you balanced. Sometimes you feel dizzy after you stop moving. This happens because the liquid inside the ear has carried on moving for a few moments.

Without ears, people wouldn't be able to balance on their hands like this!

What noises are too loud?

Most people can hear a range of sounds – from a pin drop to a thunderclap. Sound is measured in decibels (dB). Sounds over 90 to 100 decibels can damage hearing if they continue for a long time.

Sounds	Decibels (dB)
Complete silence	0 dB
Leaves rustling	10 dB
Watch ticking	20 dB
Whisper	30 dB
Normal conversation	50–60 dB
Traffic	70 dB
Lawnmower	95 dB
Chainsaw	110 dB
Music in a disco	120 dB
Thunderclap	120 dB
Jet engine	130 dB

Why Do Tummies Rumble?

Tummies rumble because of the way the body digests food. If you stretched out the human **digestive system** it would make a tube 10 m (33 ft) long. **Muscles** move food through your digestive system by squeezing and relaxing the tubes. This movement makes a rumbling noise, which sounds even louder when the stomach is empty.

Why is fibre good for you?

Fibre is good for you because it helps you to digest your food. Some foods we eat contain fibre. As fibre passes through the digestive system it soaks up water. This helps to make food move through the intestine more quickly. Fibre also makes faeces (poo) softer and easier to pass.

Wholegrain foods such as wholemeal bread, brown rice, or wholemeal pasta are good sources of fibre.

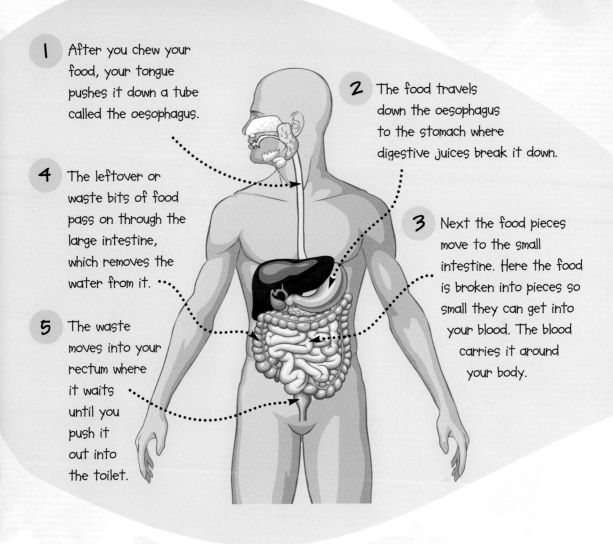

1 After you chew your food, your tongue pushes it down a tube called the oesophagus.

2 The food travels down the oesophagus to the stomach where digestive juices break it down.

4 The leftover or waste bits of food pass on through the large intestine, which removes the water from it.

3 Next the food pieces move to the small intestine. Here the food is broken into pieces so small they can get into your blood. The blood carries it around your body.

5 The waste moves into your rectum where it waits until you push it out into the toilet.

Why do poos smell?

Poos smell because of bacteria in your intestines. Bacteria eat some of the wastes that your body doesn't need. Bacteria are incredibly tiny living things, and like other living things they produce waste. Their wastes are gases and chemicals that smell. When they mix with the wastes in your intestine they make your poo smell, too.

How Do Bodies Move?

Bodies move because muscles pull on the bones in the **skeleton**. Bones cannot move by themselves. They only move when the brain sends signals to muscles telling them to move.

How do muscles work?

Muscles work in pairs because they can only pull in one direction. To bend the arm, the muscle on top of the upper arm has to contract. This means that it tightens and pulls the lower arm upwards. When this muscle relaxes, another muscle on the underside of the upper arm pulls the lower arm down. This straightens the arm. You should be able to feel the muscles contract and relax when you bend and straighten your arm.

Weightlifters make their arm muscles bigger and stronger by using the muscles to lift heavy weights regularly.

What are joints?

Joints are places where bones meet. Bones are hard and rigid, so they cannot bend. Joints connect the bones and bones move at joints.

The bones at a joint are held in place by stretchy bands called ligaments. These hold the bones tightly, but allow them to move as well.

The ball-and-socket joints in your shoulders allow you to swing your arms all around.

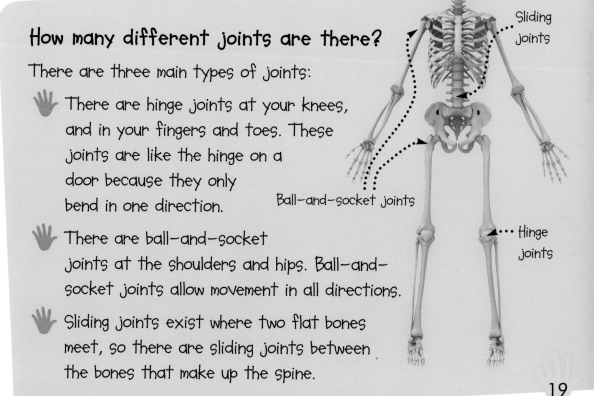

How many different joints are there?

There are three main types of joints:

There are hinge joints at your knees, and in your fingers and toes. These joints are like the hinge on a door because they only bend in one direction.

There are ball-and-socket joints at the shoulders and hips. Ball-and-socket joints allow movement in all directions.

Sliding joints exist where two flat bones meet, so there are sliding joints between the bones that make up the spine.

Sliding joints

Ball-and-socket joints

Hinge joints

19

How Do People Grow?

People grow by increasing the number of **cells** in their body. The body is made up of millions of tiny cells. Similar kinds of cells grow together to form different body parts. For example, skin cells form skin and just 1 sq cm (0.15 sq in) of skin contains about 7 million skin cells!

What do bodies need to grow?

At least five portions of fruit and vegetables a day because these contain vitamins and minerals, which you need to be healthy.

Plenty of starchy foods such as bread, rice, pasta, and potatoes for energy.

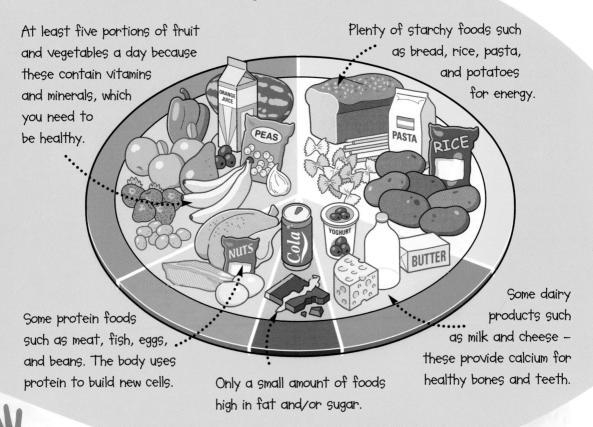

Some protein foods such as meat, fish, eggs, and beans. The body uses protein to build new cells.

Only a small amount of foods high in fat and/or sugar.

Some dairy products such as milk and cheese — these provide calcium for healthy bones and teeth.

What is puberty?

Puberty is one of two times in a person's life when they grow faster than usual. The other time is in a baby's first year. Puberty happens any time between the ages of about eight to 18. As well as growing taller during puberty, children also start to become adults. This means other body changes happen, such as girls developing a curvy, woman's shape and boys growing hair on their face.

When do people stop growing?

People stop growing when they reach adulthood, which is at about the age of 20. This is when bones stop growing longer so people stop getting taller. After this age, the body still needs fuel for energy and to replace worn-out cells or repair damaged ones. In fact 50,000 of the cells in your body will have died and been replaced with new cells while you were reading this sentence!

The human body changes in size and shape as people grow from babies into adults.

21

Glossary

auditory process of hearing

brain organ inside the skull that controls how the body works

cell building block of all living things

digestive system the food processing system of the body, including the mouth, teeth, stomach, and intestines

enamel hard, white substance covering the teeth

joint place where two bones meet

muscle tissue in the body that contracts (tightens) to cause movement of bones and other body parts

nerve thin strand carrying messages between one part of the body and another

nervous system nerve network that carries messages from the brain to the rest of the body

organ part of the body with a particular function. For example, the heart, that pumps blood around the body

oxygen gas in the air that people and other animals need to breathe in to release energy from food

particles tiny pieces of something

receptor special nerve ending that converts a movement into a signal

signal electrical message

skeleton all the bones of the body that link together to provide the framework that supports the body and gives it its shape

sound wave vibrations, rather like ripples in a pond, that carry sound through air and other materials

Further Information

Websites

Find out more about the human body at:
www.bbc.co.uk/science/humanbody

Test yourself with quizzes, word finds, and activities about the human body at:
www.kidshealth.org/kid/htbw

Learn all about what your brain does to make your body work at:
www.sciencemuseum.org.uk/on-line/brain

Books

Body: An Amazing Tour of Human Anatomy by Robert Winston. Dorling Kindersley (2005).

Human Body (Navigators) by Miranda Smith. Kingfisher (2008).

Life Processes by Richard and Louise Spilsbury. Heinemann Library (2004).

Index